DR. CIRCUIT

The Furry Therapist

A real story by:

Kavita (Milli) Jain

INDIA · SINGAPORE · MALAYSIA

ISBN 979-8-89961-981-6

Dedication

To Circuit, the little soul who changed our lives forever.

To my son, Darsh, whose heart beats with the purest love.

To my daughter, whose heart understand animals more deeply than words can express, who connects with their silence more than with human noise.

This book is lovingly dedicated to my father, Late K.P. Agarwal, who gave us our first pet – and with it, the gift of trust, care, and unconditional love.

To all the silent voices that deserve to be heard, loved, and protected.

Epigraph

"Until one has loved an animal, a part of one's soul remains unawakened."

– Anatole France

Contents

Foreword 6
Introduction 7
Author's Notes 8

Chapter 1   The Wild Visitor Who Stayed 10

Chapter 2   More Than a Monkey 14

Chapter 3   The Happiness Magnet 21

Chapter 4   A Trusting Heart in a Cruel World 25

Chapter 5   The Unanswered Call 29

Chapter 6   The Eternal Bond 32

Chapter 7   Circuit's Legacy: A Plea for Kindness 36

Chapter 8   Was Circuit Really Bal Hanuman? 40

Chapter 9   A Message from Little Circuit to All the Little Wonders 45

Chapter 10   Best of Buddies 48

Chapter 11   The Day Circuit Communicated through an Animal Communicator 53

Chapter 12   Stories from Admirers 57

Foreword

"This book is more than just a story; it is a heartfelt plea for kindness, a reminder that animals are not just creatures who exist alongside us, but sentient beings who love, trust, and feel just as deeply as we do. Kavita has woven an extraordinary tale—one that will resonate with anyone who has ever shared a true bond with an animal."

Mayank Jain

Introduction

"Circuit was more than just a monkey; he was a presence, a light, a soul that touched our hearts in ways we never imagined. This book is not just his story—it is a journey of love, loss, and the lessons he left behind. As you turn these pages, I hope you find in Circuit a reflection of the unconditional love that animals bring into our lives, and I hope his story inspires you to see them not just as creatures, but as kindred spirits who deserve our kindness."

Author's Notes

Every so often, life gifts us with a presence so pure, so full of boundless energy and love, that it leaves an everlasting imprint on our hearts. Circuit was one such blessing. A tiny, mischievous, and affectionate baby monkey who became an inseparable part of our lives, bringing with him laughter, lessons, and love that transcended species.

Circuit was more than just an animal companion; he was family. His playful antics, deep expressive eyes, and the way he formed bonds with every member of our home made him special. But perhaps, what touched us the most was his unwavering innocence and trust—qualities that reminded me of Bal Hanuman.

The tale of Bal Hanuman is one of divine mischief, immense strength, and an unshakable connection with love and devotion. As a child, Hanuman embodied curiosity and boundless energy, sometimes leading him into delightful chaos, yet always radiating an aura of purity and affection. Circuit, in his own way, mirrored these traits. His boundless enthusiasm, playful mischief, and deep emotional intelligence often reminded me of the stories of young Hanuman, whose innocence and strength made him beloved by all.

Writing this book has been my way of honouring Circuit's presence in our lives. It is a tribute to the love he shared and the lessons he taught us about kindness, patience, and the joy of living in the moment.

I hope this book brings you warmth and reminds you of the profound connections we share with all living beings. Circuit may have been a little monkey, but his love was immense—a love that, like the spirit of Bal Hanuman, remains eternal.

Chapter 1

The Wild Visitor Who Stayed

Some encounters in life are like whispers from the universe, quiet yet profound. They arrive unexpectedly, unsettling the usual rhythm of life, only to weave themselves into the very fabric of our existence. That is how Circuit came into my world—not as a pet, not as a passing visitor, but as something more, something unspoken yet deeply understood.

It was an ordinary day, painted with the usual sights and sounds of our neighbourhood. The trees swayed gently, their leafy fingers brushing against the rooftops, and the distant hum of daily life provided the usual backdrop. But amidst this routine, a lively chaos broke through—a troop of monkeys had arrived. They came with boundless energy, leaping in our balcony grill to another, skidding across terraces, and chattering in their own animated language.

Most were fleeting guests, their presence lasting only as long as their curiosity, but one tiny figure lingered—watching, waiting, studying.

At first, he was just another baby monkey, blending into the troop, but something about him demanded a second look. He wasn't merely restless like the others; he was observant, cautious. His tiny hands would reach out, grasping the edges of familiarity before recoiling into uncertainty. He studied me with an intensity that belied his small form, his bright eyes filled with both mischief and something deeper—a silent question.

First Steps Toward Trust

Trust, especially in the wild, is not given freely. It is earned, step by careful step, like the way Bal Hanuman first won the trust of the sages in the ashrams of ancient forests. Much like the young Vanara prince who curiously observed the rishis before playfully interacting with them, Circuit too was testing the waters, gauging if this new presence—me—could be trusted.

Our first interaction was hesitant, like the first steps of a dance where neither partner knows the rhythm yet. I offered him a slice of apple, my fingers stretching forward with careful patience. He didn't grab it right away. Instead, he observed me, tilting his little head as if weighing his decision. Trust is not something that comes easily to wild creatures, and I knew I had to earn it. Slowly, tentatively, he reached out. His tiny fingers brushed against mine as he took the apple, and in that single touch, I felt something stir in me—a quiet joy, an unspoken promise.

From that moment on, it became our little ritual. Every morning, I would leave a small offering—sometimes fruit, sometimes nuts—and he would wait, watching from a distance before inching closer. Each day, his hesitation faded a little more, until one morning, he didn't wait at all. He simply scampered toward me, as if he had already decided—I trust you.

A hesitant step. A pause. Another step. Then, in one swift motion, he grabbed the fruit and scrambled back to the safety of the tree's embrace. He didn't eat it immediately; instead, he held it, observing me once again, as if weighing the fairness of this exchange.

This dance of patience continued for days. Each morning he would inch a little closer. Until, one day, he did not wait—he approached with newfound confidence, took the fruit from my fingers, and in doing so, crossed the invisible threshold that separated the wild from the familiar. That was the day I knew he wasn't just another wild monkey. He had chosen me, just as much as I had chosen him.

A Name That Matched the Spirit

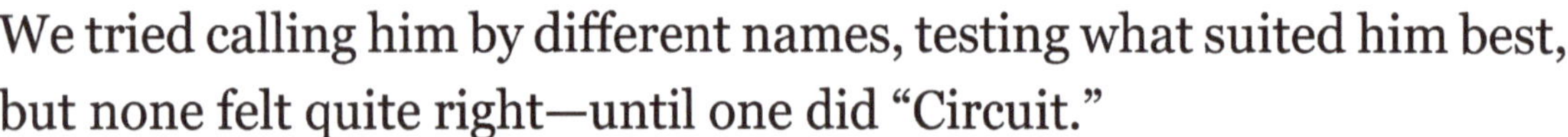

Naming is a powerful act. It solidifies presence, transforms the nameless into the known. But finding the right name is not always easy.

We tried calling him by different names, testing what suited him best, but none felt quite right—until one did "Circuit."

It fit him in a way that no other name could. He was restless, full of boundless energy, always in motion like an electric current that never ceased. One moment, he was perched quietly on a branch, and the next, he was leaping onto my shoulder, making me laugh with his sudden, unpredictable movements. He was quick, mischievous, unpredictable—yet incredibly endearing. The moment the name was uttered, it felt right.

Circuit.

Quick, erratic, full of life—his movements mirrored his name, as though he had been waiting all along for someone to simply recognize what he had always been.

And with a name, he became something more than just another monkey in the troop. He became an individual. A presence in our home, in our lives, in our hearts.

The Silent Approval

Animals do not speak in our language, yet they communicate in ways far deeper than words. Circuit's parents, ever watchful, had observed this growing bond, and though they never intervened, their approval came in the subtlest of ways.

They no longer pulled him away when he reached out for the fruit I offered. They did not discourage his presence near me. In the quiet way of nature, they acknowledged that I meant him no harm. Perhaps they saw what I myself was only beginning to understand—this was no mere fascination between a human and an animal. This was something else, something ancient and instinctual, a connection that needed no explanation.

Lessons from a Tiny Monkey

Bal Hanuman, in his childhood mischief, often formed unexpected bonds—be it with sages, celestial beings, or even the elements themselves. His playfulness was never just about amusement; it was an expression of his nature, his boundless love for the world around him. Circuit, in his own small way, mirrored this spirit.

He was wild yet familiar, untamed yet trusting. He moved between two worlds—the jungle and my home—without truly belonging to either, much like Hanuman before realizing his divine purpose. He taught me patience, for trust cannot be rushed. He taught me understanding, for communication does not always need words. And above all, he taught me that love is not bound by species or spoken promises—it simply is.

A Wild Visitor Who Stayed

Before Circuit, monkeys had always been part of the background, their presence a momentary amusement rather than a personal connection. But he changed that. He was not just another wild creature passing through; he had become part of our story, carving out a place for himself in the spaces between expectation and serendipity.

Many would ask why I grew so attached, why he mattered so much. The answer was simple—because some bonds are not chosen, they are destined. Circuit had arrived unannounced, much like the mischievous, ever-curious Bal Hanuman leaping toward the rising sun, driven by instinct rather than reason.

And just like that divine child, Circuit had unknowingly illuminated a new understanding in my heart—a reminder that sometimes, the most profound connections in life come not from seeking, but from allowing them to unfold in their own time, in their own way.

He had come as a visitor, but he stayed as family.

* * * * *

Chapter 2

More Than a Monkey

Some bonds form in silence, through a series of unnoticed moments. And then there are those that crash into your life with the force of a summer storm—loud, unexpected, and impossible to ignore. Circuit was the latter.

From the beginning, there was something undeniably different about him. He wasn't just another baby monkey swinging from branches or stealing fruits like the others. He carried himself with an uncanny intelligence, a sense of mischief that felt deliberate, almost calculated. He was, in every sense, a character—an individual, not just an animal.

The Knowing Eyes

It wasn't just his mischief that set him apart—it was his eyes. They held a depth, a spark of intelligence that made it impossible to see him as just another animal. His gaze was knowing, almost as if he understood the world in a way we couldn't.

Whenever I sat alone, lost in thought, Circuit would appear. Sometimes he would simply sit beside me, his tiny fingers brushing against my arm as if to say, *I'm here.* Other times, he would tap my face insistently until I snapped out of my thoughts.

"Alright, Circuit, what is it now?" I would ask, laughing.

He would respond by hopping onto my lap, inspecting my hands, as if ensuring that I was alright. That was his way—expressing concern without words, making sure I never stayed lost in my worries for too long.

Dr. Circuit: The Self-Appointed Healer

One of Circuit's most peculiar habits was his fascination with "checking" on me. He would carefully examine my fingers, my ears, my eyes, sometimes even peering into my mouth as if trying to diagnose something.

"Dr. Circuit at your service," I teased, as he placed a tiny hand on my forehead, his face scrunched in deep concentration. His daily routine included inspecting my clothes, pulling at my sleeves, and occasionally tapping my nose—perhaps to confirm that it was still in place.

The title stuck. From that day on, whenever he performed one of his "medical checkups," we would call him Dr. Circuit. The funniest part was how seriously he took his role. If I pretended to be unwell, he would rush to my side, poking my cheeks and sniffing my hands, his concern unmistakable. He had a way of looking at me, tilting his head as if to say, What's wrong? I'm here. And just like that, the heaviness in my heart would lift.

There is a reason animals are known to be natural healers. Studies talk about the therapeutic benefits of spending time with animals—how they lower stress, reduce anxiety, and bring comfort in ways that even words cannot. But I didn't need studies to tell me that. I had Circuit. His warmth, his presence, his tiny arms wrapping around me in an embrace—I had never known that something so small could hold so much love.

Circuit was a magician, a mind read, a healer and my friend too. A soul that entered my life when I needed him the most—even before I realized it myself. And so , I gave him title that suited him perfectly "Dr. Circuit"

With medical degree... The **Circuit Certification of Instant Happiness**." And his treatment -Endless cuddles, playful antics, and an unconditional love that had the power to heal even the heaviest hearts.

He has his own way of treating starting the day with the blessing and with through check-up and then followed by his own magical ways.

🐒 **Dr. Circuit's Daily Prescription** 🩺

Patient: My Favorite Human 🧡

Doctor on Duty: *Dr. Circuit, Chief of Monkey Medicine*

🔷 **Morning Routine Check-up:**

✅ *Blessings First* – Because good vibes heal everything!

✅ *Teeth Inspection* – No cavities? Great, now smile! 😁

✅ *Nose Check* – Sniff, sniff... hmm, all clear! 👃

✅ *Ear Examination* – Listening to my tiny doctor? Good! 👂

✅ *Eye Test* – Blink twice if you're ready for fun! 👀

💊 **Diagnosis:** 100% fit for love and mischief!

🎉 **Treatment:** Unlimited monkey hugs, playful jumps & a lifetime supply of joy!

🐵 *Dr. Circuit says: "Laughter is the best medicine, but monkey cuddles work even better!"* 🧡

Circuit the Acrobat

Circuit's energy knew no limits. One second he would be curled up beside me, the next, he would launch himself into the air, swinging effortlessly between branches. His movements were so fluid, so precise, that it often seemed like he was defying gravity.

Watching him, I was reminded of another tale from Bal Hanuman's childhood—the time he playfully tied up the demons sent to stop him, wrapping them up in his tail with such speed that they never saw it coming. Circuit had that same unstoppable spirit. No obstacle was too big, no leap too daring.

One day, he decided to test his skills by leaping from the edge of the balcony onto the clothesline. The thin rope wobbled, but Circuit balanced effortlessly, swaying back and forth with pure delight. Then, with a flick of his tail, he performed a perfect somersault mid-air and landed gracefully on the ground, looking at me as if expecting applause.

"That's it," I said. "You're officially the daredevil of the house."

The Language We Created

Despite never speaking a word, Circuit had an entire vocabulary of gestures, sounds, and expressions. Over time, we developed our own form of communication.

If he wanted food, he would sit near me, raising one eyebrow expectantly. He would express through actions by opening the door of the cupboard and the cap of his desired dry fruit bottle . If he wanted attention, he would jump on my head . If he was upset, he would cross his arms and turn away in dramatic fashion, peeking back occasionally to see if I had noticed his sulking. And then there were his playful tricks. If I was busy with something, he would snatch an object— and run just far enough to make me follow. As soon as I got close, he would drop it and dart away, his laughter evident in the way his tiny shoulders shook.

　Dr. Circuit

A Presence Larger Than Life

Circuit wasn't just a monkey. He was a force of nature, a burst of energy that filled every moment with laughter, curiosity, and unexpected lessons.

He taught me to pay attention—to the small joys, to the unspoken bonds, to the moments of pure, uncomplicated happiness. He reminded me that life isn't just about moving forward, but about stopping, playing, and savouring the adventure.

I often found myself looking over my shoulder, expecting to see him watching me with that mischievous glint in his eye. And when I did, he was always there—tail flicking, eyes twinkling, ready to pull me into yet another wild, wonderful adventure.

He was magic in its purest, most playful form.

* * * * *

Chapter 3

The Happiness Magnet

Circuit was a force of nature—a tiny bundle of boundless energy and unfiltered joy. Unlike the measured, restrained happiness humans sometimes exhibit, Circuit's enthusiasm was pure, spilling over onto everyone he met. He found happiness in the simplest things: the rustling of leaves, the taste of ripe fruit, the warmth of a familiar hand. And just like Bal Hanuman, whose mischief was never mere trouble but a playful expression of his divine energy, Circuit's antics brought people together in the most unexpected ways.

A Morning Ritual of Joy

Every morning, as the first rays of sunlight kissed the treetops, Circuit would perform his grand entrance. He had a habit of leaping onto the veranda railing and peering inside, waiting for his human family to notice him. The moment their eyes met his, he would let out an excited chitter, as if saying, "Finally! You're awake!" It was impossible not to smile at his delight.

Every morning, I made it a point to rise early, rushing through my tasks just so I could carve out time for him. And on the days I hadn't finished yet—well, the moment I saw him, everything else could wait. I would drop it all, just to be with him. It always felt like a reunion after days apart, even if it had only been a few hours. There was this silent understanding between us, a deep love that waited patiently each day for the moment we could be together again.

He was the beginning of my day, the brightest part of it. His presence filled me with so much joy that I found myself moving through chores faster, more focused—because

in the back of my mind, there was always that quiet urgency. The thought that if I missed even one chance to play with him, to share a moment, it would be gone forever. And no amount of time later could make up for it. Every day felt like a precious gift, and I didn't want to waste even a second of it without him.

A Mischief Maker with a Golden Heart

Much like Bal Hanuman, whose childhood pranks often carried a deeper meaning, Circuit's mischief was never without joy. His playful nature wasn't about causing trouble—it was his way of spreading laughter and connecting with us. He was infamous for sneaking into the kitchen, not to steal food, but to collect curious little "treasures" that fascinated him. A rubber band, a piece of cloth, a shiny spoon—these were his prized possessions, carefully hidden away in his secret stash.

His happiness lived in the smallest things. He had a quirky fondness for my glasses—often pulling them off with his tiny fingers and examining them with great interest. Sometimes, he'd sit quietly, eyes fixated on my jewellery, mesmerized by the sparkle and movement. His curiosity was endless, innocent, and full of wonder. In every act of mischief, there was an unspoken affection—a reminder that love doesn't always come in grand gestures, but in these quiet, playful moments.

Lessons in Laughter and Lightness

If Circuit had one mission in life, it was to remind people not to take things too seriously. He had an uncanny ability to sense when someone was upset, and instead of offering quiet comfort, he opted for distraction.. If someone sat in silence, lost in thought, he would gently tug at their sleeve until they acknowledged him. His joy was persistent, unrelenting—almost as if he refused to allow sadness in his presence. Circuit's magic wasn't just limited to those who saw him in person. Even people who watched his videos or heard his stories felt an instant connection.

Strangers who had never met him messaged me to say that just seeing him play made their day better. That in a world full of stress and uncertainty, this tiny monkey had managed to bring them a moment of peace, of happiness.

Celebrating the Little Things

Circuit celebrated life in its smallest details. The way he reacted to a sudden gust of wind—leaping into the air as if trying to catch it—or the way he played with falling leaves, treating them like treasures, was a lesson in itself. He found joy in things humans often overlooked.

This reminded everyone of the tales of Bal Hanuman, who once mistook the sun for a ripe fruit and leaped toward it with unwavering confidence. Like Hanuman, Circuit had an insatiable curiosity and a knack for making the ordinary extraordinary. He was a living reminder that happiness didn't always come from grand achievements; sometimes, it was found in chasing a butterfly or balancing on a fence post just to feel the wind.

An Unspoken Connection

For all his mischief, Circuit had a depth to him that made people pause. His ability to spread joy wasn't just about the things he did—it was about the way he made people feel. He had a way of making everyone believe, if only for a moment, that they were part of something magical.

Whether it was a child learning to laugh again after a bad day, a lonely neighbour finding companionship, or a household waking up to a little more excitement, Circuit's presence was undeniable. He wasn't just a monkey—he was a happiness magnet, a tiny, furry reminder of the purest form of joy.

And in a world where people often forgot how to play, how to laugh without restraint, Circuit was there to remind them, one leap at a time.

* * * * *

Chapter 4

A Trusting Heart in a Cruel World

Some souls radiate love so purely that it seems as though the world should naturally embrace them. But, as fate often shows, the world can be harshest to those who least deserve cruelty. Circuit was one of those rare beings—overflowing with joy, trust, and innocence. Yet, trust in a world that does not always return it can be both a gift and a curse.

His journey, though filled with love and laughter, was not without trials. Despite being a source of boundless happiness, he had to navigate a world that often viewed him as nothing more than a nuisance. And in those struggles, Circuit became more than just a little monkey—he became a lesson in resilience, a reminder of how even the purest hearts must sometimes endure pain.

The Innocence That Knew No Fear

Circuit was different from the rest of his troop. While they were cautious, he was curious. Where they hesitated, he leaped forward, fearless and full of wonder. His world was not divided into friend and foe; to him, every outstretched hand was a gesture of kindness, every human a potential friend.

When he heard a warm voice, he would rush toward it with no hesitation. If someone extended a hand, he would reach out his tiny fingers, believing in the goodness of the world. Unlike humans, who are taught to be wary, Circuit's heart was open. And that openness, that boundless trust, was both his strength and his greatest vulnerability.

But not everyone saw Circuit the way I did.

The Silent Worries of His Parents

Circuit's parents, wise and watchful, had an instinct he lacked—they knew that humans were unpredictable. Every time he bounded toward a stranger, his mother's sharp eyes followed. His father would always stay close, ready to intervene. They had learned, perhaps from bitter experience, that humans could be kind, but they could also be cruel.

Yet, with me, they made an exception. They let Circuit run into my arms, let him play and climb onto my shoulders, as if sensing that, with me, he was safe. But their ever-watchful presence reminded me of a sad truth—Circuit's trust was not always a gift in this world.

When Love Wasn't Enough

For all the love Circuit gave, not everyone welcomed him. To some, he was not a playful spirit, not a friend, not a healer—he was simply an inconvenience. They did not see his innocence, only his mischief. They did not understand his curiosity, only his intrusion.

If he climbed onto a balcony, searching for food, he was seen as a thief. If he played on a rooftop, leaping with joy, he was labelled a nuisance. If he nibbled on leaves or tasted fruit left unattended, he was a menace.

And they wanted him gone.

The Hypocrisy of Humans

The irony of it all struck me hard. The same people who chased Circuit away were the ones who sought peace in nature, who admired wildlife from a distance, clicking pictures with exotic animals. They spoke of the beauty of the wild, but when nature knocked at their doorstep in the form of a small, innocent being, they turned away.

A monkey in a distant sanctuary was majestic. A monkey in their backyard was a pest.

This realization hurt more than I expected. How could love be conditional? How could admiration exist only at a distance?

The Cruelty He Endured

I had seen kindness, but I had also seen the other side of human nature.

Circuit, with his trusting heart, became an easy target for those who did not see him as I did. Water was thrown at him to drive him away. Stones were hurled to make him run. He was shooed, yelled at, and hit—simply for existing.

One evening, I found him sitting near my door, shivering. His tiny body was drenched, his fur clinging to his trembling frame. Someone had thrown a bucket of water at him, and he had no idea why. He looked up at me, eyes wide, confused.

Why?

How do you explain human cruelty to a being who only knows love?

Even then, he did not lash out. He did not bite, scratch, or retaliate. Despite being hurt, he remained the same—loving, trusting, forgiving.

A Reflection of Bal Hanuman

In many ways, Circuit reminded me of *Bal Hanuman*—playful yet powerful, innocent yet wise. Like the little Hanuman who innocently mistook the sun for a ripe fruit, Circuit too was fearless, believing in the goodness of the world.

And like Hanuman, he faced misunderstanding and rejection. Hanuman's strength lay in his boundless energy and devotion, and Circuit's lay in his unwavering trust. But while Hanuman had the power of a deity to protect him, Circuit had only his resilience. His was a battle fought not with might, but with silent endurance.

Who Is Truly More Evolved?

There were days when I wondered—who was truly more evolved?

Those who claimed intelligence, yet lacked compassion? Or the one who had no words, yet understood love better than any of us?

Circuit never changed, no matter how the world treated him. Even on days when he was hurt, he would still return to me, still leap into my lap, still offer his tiny hands as if saying, *It's okay. I still love you.*

And in those moments, I realized—his soul was far greater than ours.

The Silent Strength of the Smallest Creatures

Circuit taught me that strength is not always about fighting back. Sometimes, it is in choosing love over anger. In remaining kind in a world that isn't.

He faced challenges that no small creature should have to face. Yet, he remained joyful. He remained pure. And that, to me, made him a hero—not the kind that wears a cape, but the kind that lives with an open heart, despite knowing the risk. The kind that chooses love, even when love is not returned.

And that is why, despite everything, Circuit was never just a monkey.

He was a lesson. A reminder. A light. A soul far ahead of human hearts and minds.

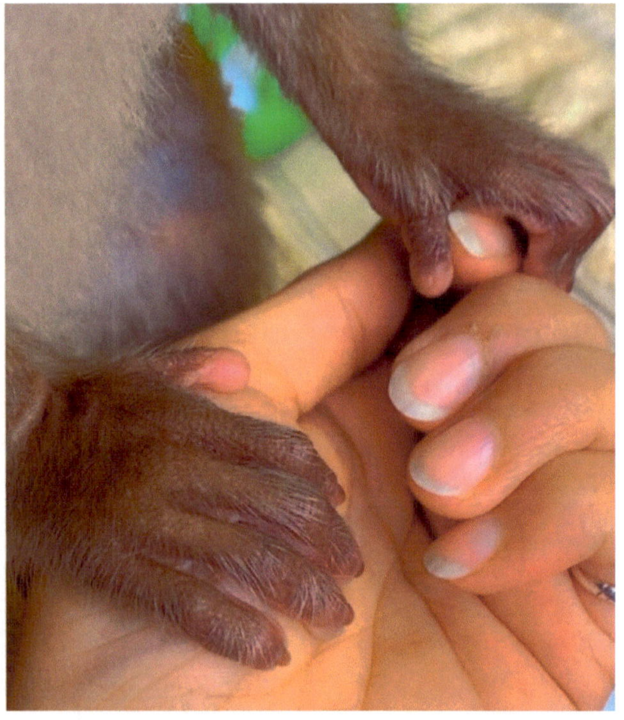

* * * * *

Chapter 5

The Unanswered Call

It started like any other day. The sun filtered through the trees, casting golden streaks across the courtyard where Circuit usually began his morning mischief. But that day, something was different. The air carried an unusual stillness, a quiet that felt almost unnatural.

I called out his name, expecting to hear the usual rustling of leaves, the sound of his tiny feet scampering along the boundary wall, or—if I was lucky—his mischievous little leap straight onto my shoulder. But there was nothing. Just silence.

At first, I thought he was playing a game. After all, Circuit loved to tease me, hiding behind flower pots or climbing to the highest branches just to see how long it would take me to find him. I could almost hear his chattering laughter in my mind.

"Circuit!" I called again, my voice echoing into the morning air.

Nothing

A slight unease settled in my chest. I walked around the house, checking all his favourite spots. I took my kids up to the rooftop, our hearts heavy with hope and worry. We searched every corner, calling out his name again and again—softly at first, then louder, as if our voices could draw him out from his favourite hiding spots. We looked in all the places where he usually spent his time, the nooks that once echoed with his playful presence. But this time, there was no rustle, no familiar leap, no tiny face peeking out.

Only silence answered us.

A deep, aching stillness filled the space where his energy once danced. The rooftop, once alive with joy and mischief, now felt hollow. It was as if the whole world had paused, holding its breath with us.

I grabbed a banana—his favourite treat—and stood near my balcony, the way I always did to call him home. The sound usually worked like magic, pulling him from wherever he was hiding. But the banana remained untouched in my palm.

Panic surged through me. Where was he?

I ran to all the corners of my building, my breath shallow. Had someone taken him? Had he ventured too far and lost his way? The thoughts clawed at my mind, each one more terrifying than the last.

I sprinted down the lane, calling his name at every turn. The housekeeping stuff of the building were concerned seeing my search and the entire team helped me to search but they did not find any trace

My heart began to race. This wasn't like him. Circuit never stayed away for too long. Even when he wandered, he always came back, his eyes twinkling as if he had just conquered some great adventure.

A Night Without Him

That night, the house felt unbearably silent. No tiny feet scampering on the roof. No sudden leaps onto my bed. No little hands tugging at my sleeve for attention.

I sat in the balcony, staring at the empty space where he usually sat beside me, chattering away as if narrating tales of his own adventures. My heart ached with the weight of his absence.

It felt like losing a part of my soul.

In the darkness, memories flooded my mind—the first time I had met him, the way he had hesitantly placed his tiny hands in mine, the way he had slowly learned to trust, to love.

Was he safe? Was he scared? Was he looking for me too?

I closed my eyes, whispering a silent prayer. If Bal Hanuman could leap across oceans and mountains, if he could move the very elements with his strength, then surely, Circuit—his own tiny embodiment of courage and mischief—would find his way back to me.

Wouldn't he?

I clung to that hope. Because without it, the silence would be unbearable.

And so, I waited. And prayed. And called his name one more time into the night.

"Circuit... please come back."

* * * * *

The Eternal Bond

Circuit's departure remains a mystery—one my heart still struggles to comprehend. It felt as though he had come into my life with a purpose, an old soul who knew his time was limited. Perhaps he had already planned his farewell, choosing a moment when I wasn't there to witness his final goodbye.

The Silent Goodbye

I had left for a trip, unaware that the day I stepped away, Circuit would embark on his own journey—one far beyond my reach.

When I returned, I expected to see him waiting, his playful leaps and affectionate mischief welcoming me home. Instead, silence greeted me. At first, I clung to hope, calling his name, searching for him in every corner. But soon, unease crept in—this absence was different. It carried a stillness I had never felt before.

And then, I saw his parents. Their eyes carried a knowledge I wasn't ready to accept. They moved with a sorrowful slowness, their grief unspoken but profound. The food they once eagerly shared with Circuit lay untouched—a silent tribute to the one they had lost.

Circuit was gone.

A Spirit That Never Leaves

His absence left a hollow space, yet his presence never truly faded. Some bonds are not bound by physical form.

There were moments when I felt him beside me—a whisper in the wind, a rustling in the leaves, the warm glow of the sun. Some nights, I awoke with the feeling of tiny feet brushing past me. In those moments, I whispered, "I know you're here." Because I did.

In many ways, Circuit reminded me of Bal Hanuman—mischievous, playful, yet wise beyond his form. Just like the little divine monkey who leaped toward the sun, thinking it was a fruit, Circuit had an undeniable curiosity and an unwavering spirit. And just like Bal Hanuman, he had a purpose greater than what met the eye.

Messages from Beyond

Seeking closure, I reached out to an animal communicator. Without revealing anything, I waited.

What I heard left me breathless.

"Circuit was an old soul," they said. "Wise beyond his years. His time was brief, but his impact was meant to last a lifetime."

And then, through them, he spoke to me.

"I will reconnect with you when the time is right. Stay calm. I love you deeply."

Tears blurred my vision, but a strange peace settled within me. His love had not ended—it had simply transformed.

The Final Sign

The night I left for my holy trip at 3 AM, Circuit returned one last time. He saw the children, spent a quiet moment, and then walked away. It was as if he had chosen his moment, much like great souls do.

When I returned, I took a holy dip in the Ganga for his well-being, unaware that at that very moment, I was unknowingly blessing his onward journey.

Then, came the final confirmation.

Following a trail of messages, I reached a place six kilometres away, where a guard recalled a baby monkey who had once played joyfully in the area.

"He was different," the guard said. "Friendly. Almost like he understood things. But he passed away days ago."

I didn't need more words. I knew.

Then, the guard hesitated. "I don't know why, but I kept a picture of him," he said, pulling out his phone. And there he was.

Circuit.

Even in death, he had found a way to reach me.

A Love That Crosses Lifetimes

Through the communicator, Circuit sent me one final message.

"I love you like a crisscross."

At first, I didn't understand. But then it became clear—a crisscross represents paths intertwining, merging lives, a love that never parts. He was telling me that our bond was eternal.

Bal Hanuman once carried an entire mountain when searching for Sanjeevani, not knowing exactly what he was looking for but knowing he had to try. My search for Circuit felt the same. And just like the divine child found his way, Circuit had found his way back to me, through signs, messages, and an unbreakable bond.

Living the Life He Gave Me

Grief taught me something unexpected. Instead of mourning, I should honour the life he awakened within me. Maybe that was his true purpose. Maybe that was why he came to me.

Even now, he continues to send me signs, little reminders that he is still with me. And though his physical form is gone, I believe he will return.

Because he was never just beside me.

He was within me.

And some souls—some loves—are never meant to be apart.

* * * * *

Chapter 7

Circuit's Legacy: A Plea for Kindness

The world is full of stories that never get told, voices that never get heard. Among them are the silent cries of animals—beings who love, who feel pain, who form bonds just as deeply as humans do. Yet, their struggles often go unnoticed, their existence taken for granted.

Circuit was one of those voices. But unlike so many others, his story will not be forgotten.

More Than Just an Animal

Circuit wasn't just a monkey. He was a soul that loved and trusted unconditionally. He wasn't a pet. He wasn't a stray. He was a being with emotions, with wisdom, with an extraordinary connection to the world around him. Yet, despite all the love he gave, he suffered the same fate as countless other animals who are left vulnerable in a world shaped by human desires.

Circuit and his parents once lived among humans in a so-called educated society, yet their presence was not welcomed by all. They were not seen as living beings deserving of love, space, or respect—but as inconveniences, creatures that did not belong. And so, they were driven away. Left to fend for themselves in a world that was not always kind to those without a voice.

In many ways, Circuit's story reminds us of Bal Hanuman—strong yet innocent, mischievous yet full of love. Like Hanuman's legendary childhood, Circuit had an unwavering spirit, an insatiable curiosity, and a heart so full of devotion that he never hesitated to trust. But unlike the divine Hanuman, who found protection in the gods, Circuit found himself in a world where kindness was selective, where compassion was not a given.

How Many Circuits Exist in This World?

Circuit's story is not just his. It is the story of every animal that has ever loved and lost, that has ever trusted and been betrayed, that has ever suffered in silence.

How many more like him exist? How many animals form bonds, love deeply, and yet are abandoned, neglected, or harmed—simply because they cannot protest?

And more importantly—what are we teaching our children when we turn a blind eye to such suffering?

The way we treat animals is a reflection of the values we pass down to the next generation. If a child sees an animal being kicked, ridiculed, or ignored—and no one stops to correct it—they grow up believing that such indifference is acceptable. If a child watches adults react with disgust or irritation at a stray dog seeking food, or a wounded bird in need of care, they learn that compassion is selective. That kindness is reserved only for humans.

But what if we changed that narrative?

A Lesson from Hanuman: Strength in Kindness

Bal Hanuman, in his childhood mischief, mistook the sun for a ripe fruit and tried to devour it. His innocence was limitless, his belief boundless. Even in his pranks, there was no malice—only love and curiosity. Imagine if, instead of being nurtured and guided, Hanuman had been abandoned, treated as an outcast. Would he have grown into the revered protector that the world came to admire?

Every Circuit out there has the potential for love, for loyalty, for deep and meaningful bonds. They may not have Hanuman's divine strength, but they have his unwavering heart. And it is up to us to decide whether we nurture them or cast them aside.

Justice Beyond Words: A Responsibility for All

True justice for animals is not just about feeling sorry for them. It is about action.

It is about raising children who do not turn away from suffering but extend a hand to help. It is about schools that teach respect for all lives, not just human lives. It is about a society that does not drive away a harmless creature simply because it does not fit into its rigid idea of 'belonging.'

Because every life—no matter how small, no matter how different—deserves respect.

Circuit's Message Lives On

I often wonder if Circuit came into my life to teach me this. To make me his voice. To awaken something within me that could never again be silenced. His story is not just mine to tell.

It is a story for all the animals who love and lose, who trust and are betrayed, who suffer yet continue to give. And perhaps, by listening to these unheard voices, by acknowledging their pain, we can finally begin to bring them the justice they have always deserved.

To the Parents Reading This

Teach your children compassion—not just for people, but for every living being. Teach them to care, to protect, to love beyond species. For in doing so, we do not just create kinder children—we create a kinder world.

Bal Hanuman's strength was not in his power alone, but in his unwavering devotion, his fearless love. Let us raise children who, like Hanuman, understand that true strength lies not in might, but in kindness.

Circuit may be gone, but his spirit remains. His love remains. And through this story, his voice will never be unheard again.

* * * * *

Chapter 8

Was Circuit Really Bal Hanuman?

Circuit – A Little Hanuman in My Life

Some souls are not just ordinary—they carry a spark of the divine. A presence that is larger than life, timeless, and full of purpose. Circuit was one of them.

In Sanatan Dharma, Lord Hanuman is not only known for his incredible strength but also as Bal Hanuman—the divine child, full of playfulness, devotion, and unparalleled energy.

He is considered a role model for children, teaching them about courage, kindness, innocence, and unwavering loyalty.

And just like Bal Hanuman, Circuit came into my life as a tiny, mischievous being, filling my days with love, joy, and a sense of something greater than what meets the eye.

But what made Circuit's presence even more special were the signs he gave me—the moments that made me believe he was no ordinary monkey. There was something divine about him.

The Signs of Hanuman in Circuit

From the very beginning, Circuit showed strange yet beautiful behaviours, things that no one ever taught him. They simply happened.

🛕 He always appeared on Tuesdays and Saturdays – The two days dedicated to Lord Hanuman. It was as if he knew. Even on days when he would disappear for a while, he would return on these sacred days without fail.

🍌 He loved Hanuman's prasad – His favourite foods were gud (jaggery), chana (roasted gram), tulsi (holy basil leaves), dates, and bananas—the very offerings made to Hanuman in temples. No one trained him, yet he craved the same things offered in prayers.

✨ He never missed a Tuesday treat – Every time there was a special offering, every Hanuman Jayanti, every ritual, he would be there, as if he knew it was a special occasion. He wouldn't take food on just any day, but on these days, he would sit patiently, waiting.

〽 He raised his little hands in blessing – On special occasions, he would lift his hands, just like a priest giving aashirwad (blessings). It was never taught to him, yet he did it, as if he understood the language of devotion.

📖 He sat quietly when I recited Hanuman Chalisa – It is said that when Hanuman Chalisa is recited with true devotion, Hanuman himself comes to listen. Every time I chanted, Circuit would sit still, listening, his eyes fixed on me. No jumping, no playing—just a quiet presence, as if he felt the sacred energy in the words. These weren't just coincidences. These were signs.

Signs that Circuit was not just an ordinary being.

Bal Hanuman – The Divine Protector

As a child, Bal Hanuman was known for his playful mischief.

One of the most famous stories tells how, as a little one, he leaped into the sky, mistaking the sun for a fruit. When I watched Circuit take fearless leaps, jump to impossible heights, and run without fear, I saw the same unstoppable spirit.

He was small, but his energy was boundless. He was wild, but his heart was full of love.

At times, it felt as though he carried the very essence of Hanuman himself.

Was he sent as a reminder? A message?

Or was he truly a little Hanuman in disguise?

Hanuman – The Divine Healer

Lord Hanuman is not just a protector, he is also a healer.

During the great war in Ramayana, when Lakshman was struck down by a powerful weapon, Hanuman flew to the Himalayas to fetch the Sanjeevani Booti, a divine herb that could save his life.

When he could not recognize the herb, he lifted the entire mountain and carried it back—because he could not bear the thought of failing his beloved Lord Ram and Lakshman.

📖 Circuit – My Own Sanjeevani

Just like Hanuman brought Sanjeevani to revive Lakshman, Circuit brought healing into my life. Whenever I was sad, he would sense it before I even spoke a word.

He would come to me, touch my face, play with my fingers, and sit beside me as if to say, "I'm here. You are not alone."

Whenever I felt lost, he would pull me back to the present—with his little jumps, his playful nudges, his endless energy. His presence was my medicine, his love was my Sanjeevani.

Hanuman was called Sankat Mochan, the remover of obstacles, the one who wipes away fear and sorrow. In his own small way, Circuit did the same for me.

Was Circuit a Blessing from Hanuman?

It is said that Hanuman still walks among us, appearing to those who have faith.

Some say he takes different forms, that he comes where devotion is strong and hearts are pure. Could Circuit have been a blessing from Hanuman himself?

     Dr. Circuit

Could he have been sent to remind me that faith, love, and devotion never fade?

Maybe he was not just a monkey. Maybe he was something much greater.

A Little Hanuman in My Life

Circuit came into my life like a tiny flash of lightning—bright, powerful, and unforgettable.

He was full of mischief, love, and devotion—just like Bal Hanuman.

Even though he was small, his presence was mighty.

Even though he could not speak, he taught me things no words ever could.

And even though he is gone, his spirit, his love, and his blessings will never leave me.

Because some souls, some connections, are meant to last forever.

And I will always believe—Circuit was my Bal Hanuman.

* * * * *

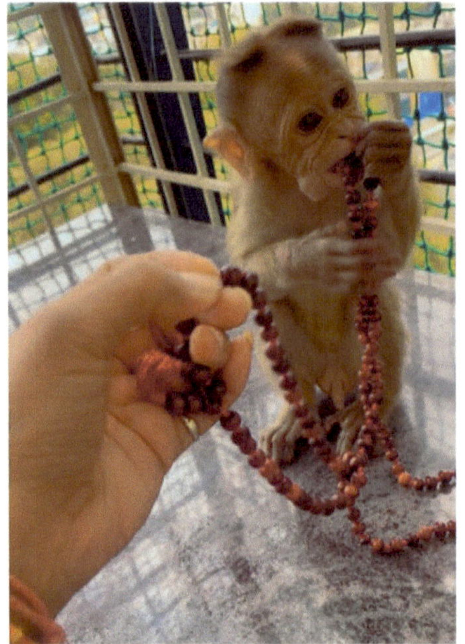
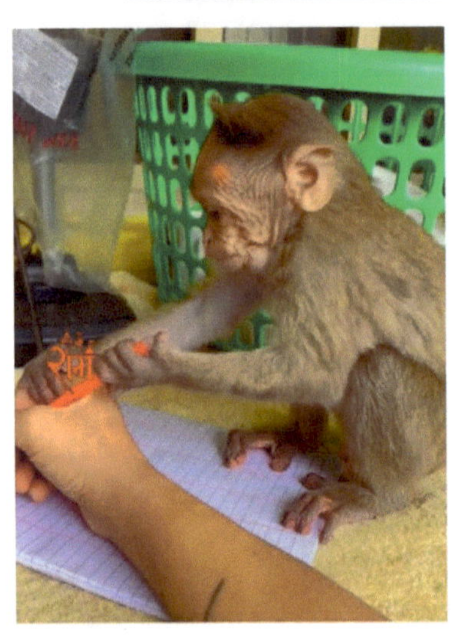

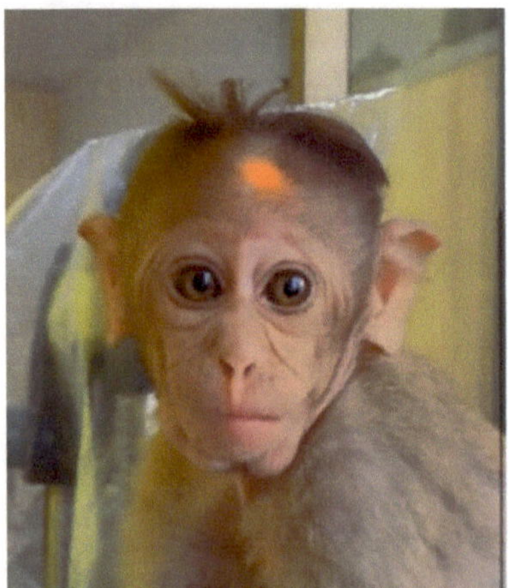

Chapter 9

A Message from Little Circuit to All the Little Wonders

Dear Little Friend,

Hi! I'm Circuit, a tiny monkey with a big heart, a playful tail, and something very special to share with you.

Our world is filled with amazing beings—people, birds, puppies, squirrels, even the tiniest ants. We may all look different, but we all have one thing in common:

We feel love, just like you.

We feel pain, just like you.

We want to feel safe, just like you.

So here's my little message for you:

♡ **Love Them Like You Want to Be Loved**

If you're lonely, wouldn't a friend make you smile?

If you're hungry, wouldn't a little snack make your day?

Animals feel that too!

They may not speak with words, but they speak with their eyes, their tails, their tiny paws—and they understand kindness.

When you love them, they love you back in the most magical ways.

🦸 Be Their Hero

If you see an animal who is hurt, scared, or being treated badly—help them.

Speak up. Stand strong. You don't need a cape to be a hero!

Even small acts—like giving food to a puppy or water to a bird—can save a life. And guess what? That kindness comes back to you too.

🧠 Teach the Grown-Ups!

Sometimes, even adults forget that animals have feelings. You can remind them gently:

"Animals feel too. Let's be kind."

You're never too small to make a big difference!

🌱 Real Learning Starts with Kindness

Math and reading are great—but the most important lesson is being kind.Kindness spreads like sunshine. When others see your love for animals, they'll want to join too!

🌍 The Future Is in Your Hands

If we don't care for animals now, one day we may only see them in books or on screens. That would be so sad.

But you—you can change that.

Promise me this, my little wonder:

🐾 *Be kind.*

🐾 *Be brave.*

🐾 *Help when you can.*

🐾 *Teach others to care.*

Together, we'll make sure the world stays full of wagging tails, chirping songs, happy paws, and real love.

With tiny hugs and a heart full of hope,

Your friend,

Circuit 🐵 ♡

*   *   *   *   *

Chapter 10

Best of Buddies

Darsh's Diary: A Friendship Beyond Words

Some friendships defy explanation. They don't fit into neat labels, and they certainly don't follow the rules of the world. Circuit was one of those friendships. He wasn't a pet, a stray, or even just an animal that happened to live with us. He was family. He was the little heartbeat that pulsed through my everyday life, the unexpected gift that turned into something irreplaceable.

From the moment I met him, I felt it. The connection. The understanding. He wasn't just another monkey swinging through the world without a care—he felt things. He understood things. He knew joy, sorrow, love, and loss. And in ways I still struggle to put into words, he understood me, too.

Circuit: My Silent Healer

There were days when I felt lost, when the world felt too heavy for my young shoulders. Disappointments, frustrations, the little wounds that life gives us without warning. On those days, I didn't need words. I didn't need solutions. I just needed Circuit.

And he always knew.

He would climb onto my shoulder, rest his tiny hands on my arm, and look at me as if to say, I see you. I'm here. He wouldn't chatter or demand my attention—he would just be there. A quiet presence, a warmth that wrapped around me like a soft, invisible hug.

I never told him my worries, but somehow, he already knew them. And in his own way, he chased them away—sometimes with his antics, sometimes just by sitting beside me, watching the world go by as if to remind me that life moves forward, no matter what.

Maybe he was my best friend. Maybe he was my guardian angel. Or maybe, just maybe, he was both.

Laughter, Everywhere

Circuit had a gift—the ability to fill any space with laughter. It didn't matter if it was our home, the garden, or even the streets beyond. He belonged everywhere because everywhere was brighter when he was there.

I remember the time he discovered his own reflection in a steel plate. He froze, tilting his head, staring at his own face as if he had just met a long-lost twin. Then, after a moment, he tried to talk to himself. Chattering, making faces, jumping back in surprise whenever his own reflection copied his moves.

I laughed so hard that my stomach hurt. And for that moment, the world had no worries—just a boy and a monkey, lost in a ridiculous, perfect moment.

That was Circuit. A happiness magnet. A living, breathing reminder that life is supposed to be felt, not just endured.

The One Who Trusted Too Much

Circuit's parents were cautious. They watched us from a distance, always keeping a safe space between them and the humans who had taken their baby in. They were wary, careful, protective.

But Circuit? He was different. He believed in us. He trusted us completely.

There was no hesitation in the way he leaped into my arms. No fear when he wrapped his little fingers around mine. No doubt in his bright, searching eyes when he looked up at me as if waiting for my next word, my next move.

He believed in kindness. He believed in love.

And I wonder—did we deserve that trust? Did the world? Or was Circuit simply too pure for the place he had been born into?

One in a Million

Circuit wasn't just another monkey. He was the monkey. The one who left footprints on my heart, the one who turned everyday moments into stories I will tell for the rest of my life.

Every morning, he would wait for me. The moment he saw me, he would leap forward, chatter excitedly, and climb onto my shoulder like I was the most important person in his world. And maybe, for him, I was.

I remember the last time he did that. The way his tiny hands gripped onto me, the way he pressed his face into my cheek. It felt like a promise—like an unspoken truth that some friendships never really end, even if the world thinks they do.

Circuit may not be here anymore. But he is still my best friend. He always will be.

Some friendships never fade. Some souls never leave.

Stuti's Diary: A Friendship Beyond Words

All He Knew Was Love

Animals may not speak our language, but they feel everything — love, fear, hunger, safety, and even sadness. Just like us, they form families, protect their babies, and respond to kindness with trust. Circuit, the little baby monkey who visited our balcony every day, reminded us how human animals can be.

Not everyone saw him the way we did. While we played with him and loved him like a family member, some people only saw a wild animal. Many were scared or simply didn't like monkeys. And that fear turned into anger — even cruelty. Complaints started in our apartment society. People wanted the monkeys "gone." They didn't think about how harmless Circuit was, or how closely his parents watched over him. They only saw something different, and reacted with rejection.

But being scared of animals doesn't give anyone the right to hurt them. There are peaceful ways to keep them out of your space — like closing doors or using nets — without needing to be cruel. After all, animals don't come to us to attack or bother us. They come for food, warmth, or shelter — often because their natural homes are gone.

It's important to remember that animals lived in these spaces long before our apartments and buildings were built. As we grow and take over more land, their options become fewer. They're not intruders — they're survivors.

Circuit's story ended in heartbreak. He trusted humans, maybe too much. One day, he climbed an electric pole near a small building and was electrocuted. He didn't know it was dangerous. He was just playing — being a baby. When he died, it hurt all of us, especially my mom, who was closest to him. But his death also taught us a lesson: kindness isn't just about love — it's also about responsibility.

If we can't help an animal, the least we can do is not harm them. Feeding them, giving them water, or simply letting them be — these small acts can mean so much. They teach children empathy, and they show the world that we are capable of compassion.

Animals may not have a voice, but we do. And it's up to us to speak for them.

* * * * *

Chapter 11

The Day Circuit Communicated through an Animal Communicator

– Gauranganakumari J. Solanki

One morning I received a message from a lady (Kavita) requesting me to connect with a baby monkey in her society who had passed on to the spirit world at a very young age. Kavita sounded rather devastated and I wondered what this little monkey (Circuit) could have done in such a short period to create such a big impact.

For my telepathic animal communication, I request for a photograph of the animal to aid the process of connecting deeper. I received Circuit's picture from Kavita and was drawn to him in complete wonderment! This is when the story began to unfold - A journey of a very old and extremely special soul.

I called Kavita immediately after and conveyed to her all that I had received in the form of visions from his soul, and that is when she opened up about her connection with him.

So far, it was more of the soul showing itself briefly, but Circuit refused to open up with messages and connect further at that moment. He kept us hanging for a long, long time...

Whenever Kavita messaged me to check if he was ready to open up, Circuit kept me feeling curious, because his answers were either "not yet", "not now", "after a couple of weeks", "tomorrow", "today I got busy, check again tomorrow". This kept going on for over one month and then the day finally arrived, phew!

Being a telepathic animal and nature communicator, I know that while communicating, the souls do mention very clearly whether they are ready to connect or not. The souls who have transitioned, especially might take some time to open up and as conveyed by them, it is the time which their humans need to grieve and accept their passing on.

Circuit's soul taught me great patience and he seemed to have enjoyed the way he kept us dancing on our toes and with this, my curiosity kept building up as I knew he is a powerful soul who I was connecting with.

The day arrived when he finally said, "I am ready to connect, but you will have to convey my messages very differently. I will dictate a letter for her and you will write". This is the first time I had a request (a kind of order actually) of this sort via my communication.

As per my personal belief as a telepathic animal communicator, I don't share messages of my communication as most of them are confidential and it's also a trust which a soul builds in you. In case the humans feel like sharing experiences, that is something I leave to them. When Kavita requested me to write about Circuit I was happy, but at the same time hesitant about what I was going to mention. On checking with Kavita and Circuit, I was given a push to share some of it here.

Having communicated for the first time with this little soul, and with Kavita, I was a little surprised by the kind of request which I had received; but nonetheless I just picked up a blank sheet of paper and he began to dictate.

Animals have no filters and are very clear on what they want and don't want.

Circuit mentioned all the little details about what Kavita would do for him, be it feeding him laddoos to clearing spaces at home. He spoke about the temple bell ringing at home to describing the kitchen which he absolutely loved. He praised Kavita's beautiful voice mentioning how he enjoyed the moments when she sang to him and he had plenty of guidance for her life too. There were personal details that he mentioned which to me made no sense at all and I kept checking with him whether he wanted me to write it and all he said is – "you have to write what I am telling you, don't put your mind to it." I surrendered entirely and wrote whatever he said which only later made complete sense to Kavita when she read the letter. This special being had a divine power to him which felt like the blessings of Lord Hanumanji.

The letter was finally complete and when I sent the letter to Kavita she mentioned about my handwriting being just like her fathers. As I conveyed the entire letter writing process and discussions with Circuit while he dictated, all she said is "that sounds just like my father."

It is a mystical world and some souls either send other souls or take rebirth when they want to re-enter our lives especially when we need them the most. Animals especially come in with a purpose into our lives and work towards fulfilling it through their journey.

At times the animal souls come back to their humans to be with them again while some choose to keep guiding them via other souls.

Circuit is of course a special soul, but also an old soul and this is something which I experience quite often. Older souls speak with great authority most of the time and their behavior too from a very young age leans more towards having been there earlier in this world, a lot more experienced.

Circuit expressed himself in various ways - he showed me visions of things, at times made me listen to the sounds and also expressed himself in written words. Through telepathic communication, animals choose to convey messages in a manner which their humans can understand. They also have a way of choosing their communicators (channels or medium) based on how their messages will be received and conveyed to their humans.

Circuit amazed Kavita with the details of his observation around the house of little things right from the drawing room decor to the kitchen utensils. The power of observation is something which must never be underestimated in animals as well as their ability to understand every word you speak even though they may choose not to listen at times.

They are grounded all the time and keep us grounded too. They absorb our energies, understand and at times reflect our health as well. Our pets of course come with guidance for us, but the forests and wild animals can be magical guides. Many of them also have a great sense of humour, just like Circuit did.

Circuit lived around the society, but both wild and free. He chose the life he did and moved on after fulfilling his purpose. I am very grateful to Kavita and to Circuit for creating a big impact in my life  and letting me experience such a beautiful form of communication, a lot of which cannot be expressed in words and that is something that I will always cherish. He's truly a magical soul, one which I have understood but there is a lot more which is still to be understood in mystical ways.

I would like to end with a message as I receive from Circuit (as he dictates) – "Tell everyone that they have no idea how tiny they look from where I am. No one has a permanent place there and they all have to move on. Each one of you has the power to change now, it's all in your hands." (he shows me his palms)

Gauranganakumari J. Solanki
themysticaljourney5@gmail.com

* * * * *

Chapter 12

Stories from Admirers

Riddhi Doshi, Child Psychologist, Parenting Counsellor, Ted Speaker

Circuit: A Little Soul with a Big Presence

There are certain beings who cross our paths and leave an imprint far beyond their time with us. Circuit was one such soul. He wasn't just a monkey; he was a bundle of joy, curiosity, and love wrapped in the tiniest form. Watching his videos, seeing his playful antics, and witnessing the gentle bond he shared with Kavita made me realize how deeply animals can touch our lives.

As someone who works closely with children and parents, I often emphasize the importance of emotional intelligence, connection, and empathy. Animals, like Circuit, are living examples of unconditional love and presence. They teach us patience, nurture our ability to care, and remind us that communication goes beyond words. In a world where we often rush past life's simplest joys, Circuit was a reminder to pause, appreciate, and love wholeheartedly.

His absence is deeply felt, but his spirit continues to inspire—reminding us all to see animals not just as creatures in our world but as souls who bring wisdom, healing, and an infinite capacity to love.

B. Naweed Ara Zaman, Delhi

Hanu, as I always called him. One day, Millie uploaded a video clip of a baby monkey. Like always, I watched it, liked it, and moved on. But then she started posting more regularly, and before I realized it, that little one had captured my heart. From simply "it," he became "Hanu," and eventually, he turned into "My Little Hanu"—a name that seemed to grow naturally over time.

Hanu would visit Millie every day, playing with her, blessing her, and then leaving. I found myself eagerly waiting for Millie's uploads, which soon became a daily ritual for both her and me. Each clip was filled with love and a bond so pure it felt as though we were all connected to Hanu.

But the cruelty of this world has taken away that tiny bundle of joy so suddenly that I still struggle to accept that Hanu is no longer with us. Yet, I am deeply grateful to Millie for capturing and sharing those precious moments. Through her, she showed us that true love does exist.

Afterword / Final Thoughts

Circuit's time with us was short, but his impact will last forever. Through his story, I hope to spread a simple but powerful message: that every life, no matter how small, matters. That love knows no boundaries—not of species, nor of time. And that in a world often too busy to notice, the greatest act of kindness is simply to see, to acknowledge, and to care.

* * * * *

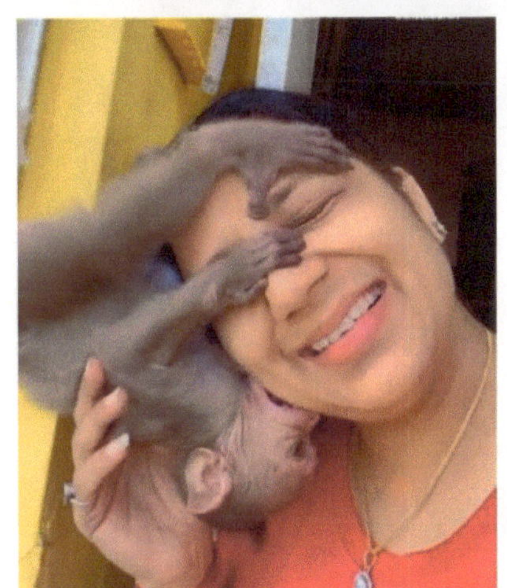

Dr. Circuit
"THE FURRY THERAPIST"
Follow for heartwarming moments.
@DR_CIRCUIT_THE_FURRY_HEALER